Field Notes
from the Hudson Valley

is a series of infrastructural investigations, essays, maps, drawings, photographs, and speculative design projects to develop provocative narratives of the condition and future of the valley, and provide a basis for planning, design and advocacy for the many stakeholders in the region.

Extending several hundred miles north from Manhattan Island, touching five states, the region includes nine counties, 13 cities and over 200 villages and towns. Its watershed covers over 13,000 square miles. The status and future of this area deeply affects the lives of millions, from New York City to a broad swath of the American northeast.

Field Notes from the Hudson Valley is a project of the Hudson Valley Initiative at Columbia University GSAPP.

Introduction

This edition of Field Notes from the Hudson Valley documents the tactical approach to activating publicly-owned vacant land through small design interventions. Invited by the City of Newburgh to prototype the temporary conversion of a city-owned lot into a neighborhood pop-up park, the Hudson Valley Initiative worked with the City and Scenic Hudson to design and build temporary structures that could be used for seating, play, picnics and to solicit feedback from neighbors about its merits. The goal was to develop a toolbox for how residents could replicate this process. In that sense, the Hudson Valley Initiative served as a 'guinea pig,' testing its capacity to build and maintain this pop-up park on a low budget and with help and input from the community along the way.

The idea of a pilot suggests to start small, that things can go wrong and we learn from failures before we scale up. Recognizing a certain level of 'Planning Fatigue' in Newburgh, the pilot was designed and assembled quickly. It wasn't preceded by a robust community engagement or design process. Instead, the pop-up park itself served as an engagement tool and feedback mechanism to inform the larger policy for utilizing city-owned vacant lots as neighbothood parks. This publication documents the process and life of the pilot between June 2018 and October 2019.

HAVE AN IDEA FOR THIS LOT?

Climing Walls
stans
leo's HOTDOGS
gans &
Auctivatys

Holy Temple U.H.C Community Park Garden

Flexible Space - Pieces

Lights
Benches

Doggie bag dispensers

Dance flor

Plants

Seating w/ Chess
Giant Checkers

Culture

Pavillion
Giant Foosball
(age appropriate)
Jungle Gym

Source: Orange County Tax Parcel Data, Field Survey by Author in 2019/2020

Vacant Land

The post-industrial American landscape contains an abundance of vacant land as a result of deindustrialization, population decline, and high foreclosure rates during the last recession. Vacant or abandoned properties are properties once used for a residential, commercial or industrial purposes, but no longer contain such use. On some, abandoned structures and building shells are a fading reminder of its past. On others, any structures or remnants of such use are erased and replaced with a low-maintenance surface such as gravel or grass.

Vacancy is primarily known as a phenomenon in distressed legacy cities like Detroit, Philadelphia, or Cleveland, with population declines of up to 60% since the mid-20th century. But many small towns and rural communities have vacancy rates that are double that of metropolitan areas according to a 2018 study by the Lincoln Institute of Land Policy.[1] No comprehensive database exists that tallies vacant land in the Hudson Valley, but it is estimated to be in the tens of thousands of acres. In a recent testimony submitted for the 2019 Joint Legislative Hearing On Economic Development, the New York Land Bank Association called these properties "zombies" – vacant and abandoned properties plaguing communities and damaging neighborhoods throughout New York State. "They can be found in just about every community in New York State, hiding in plain sight among occupied buildings and well-maintained lots, consuming municipal resources, depressing property values, reducing tax revenue, and harming surrounding residents."[2]

Catalan Architect and Historian Ignasi de Sola-Morales Rubio described the presence of urban vacant land as "internal to the city yet external to its everyday use." "[ ] they are foreign to the urban system, mentally exterior in the physical interior of the city, its negative image as much a critique as a possible alternative."[3] It is this possible alternative that evokes our imagination for dreaming up a future for these spaces, converting them once again into spaces that are internal to the city's everyday use. Whether these spaces are private property or publicly owned, citizens can play a vital role in this process of re-engaging abandoned land into their everyday life.

Newburgh, a small city 60 miles north of New York City, once a thriving industrial city on the west side of the Hudson River, has seen a dramatic decline in economic activity over the past fifty years. A loss of manufacturing jobs as well as white flight to surrounding suburbs, compounded by urban renewal in the second half of the 20th century has left the City with an astonishing inventory of over 500 vacant properties. These vacant lots and vacant building shells contribute to a perception of neglect, negatively impact the health and safety of all citizens — especially in the city's low-income communities of color — and severely reduce the city's tax base.

Many vacant properties are currently owned by the City of Newburgh –typically acquired through tax foreclosure– with little to no resources to maintain them. They attract dumping and rodents. They add a burden to the city's already strapped tax base and often contribute to a perception of blight and lack of safety. Once tax-foreclosed, vacant building shells eventually turn into vacant lots. As the structure deteriorates, it becomes a safety hazard and the city is often left with no other option but to demolish at great cost to taxpayers. The pilot at 191 South Street in Newburgh was such a site.

Foreclosed in 2009 and demolished in 2017, it now sits vacant between a church and a residential building. A recent survey of Newburgh shows 60 vacant properties within a three-block radius of the pilot site. At a nearby corner on South Street, a sea of candles reminds passersby of a life lost to gun violence. Two blocks to the north is Downing Park, a 35-acre public park designed by Frederick Law Olmsted and Calvert Vaux in 1889.[4] As with their other park designs, Olmsted and Vaux's intentions were to create open spaces to promote the well-being of the public. However apart from a dirt track up a steep hill, residents in this part of town are not offered access to Downing Park.

Numerous studies have shown the positive health and safety impacts in cities that have developed robust policies and guidelines to encourage the temporary or long-term design, improvement and programming of vacan lots.[5] Resident-led, site-specific improvements to these sites, including art installations, playgrounds, social spaces, butterfly gardens, installations that reflect on the cultural heritage or spaces that can be used for events and performances, are a pathway to empowering residents to engage in systemic change for these sites and neighborhoods. They create opportunities to test ideas, seed cultural programming and foster social cohesion among neighbors. They provide strategies for strengthening neighborhoods, where the real estate market is not able to stabilize a downward spiral of decline and neglect. Not infrequently, these sites become long-term anchors in communities contributing to positive change and at some point contested real estate.

191 South Street, Newburgh NY 12550

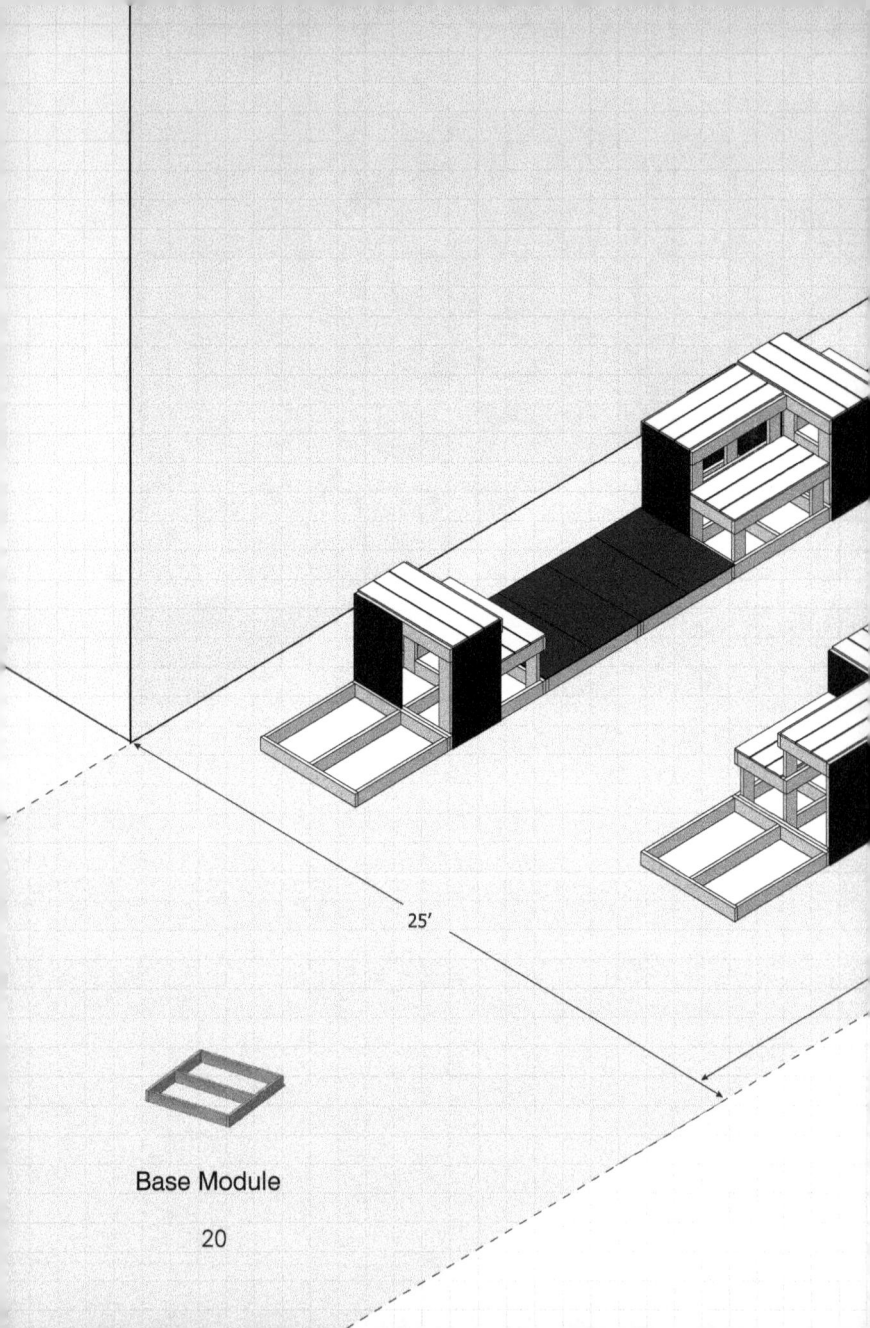

25'

Base Module

20

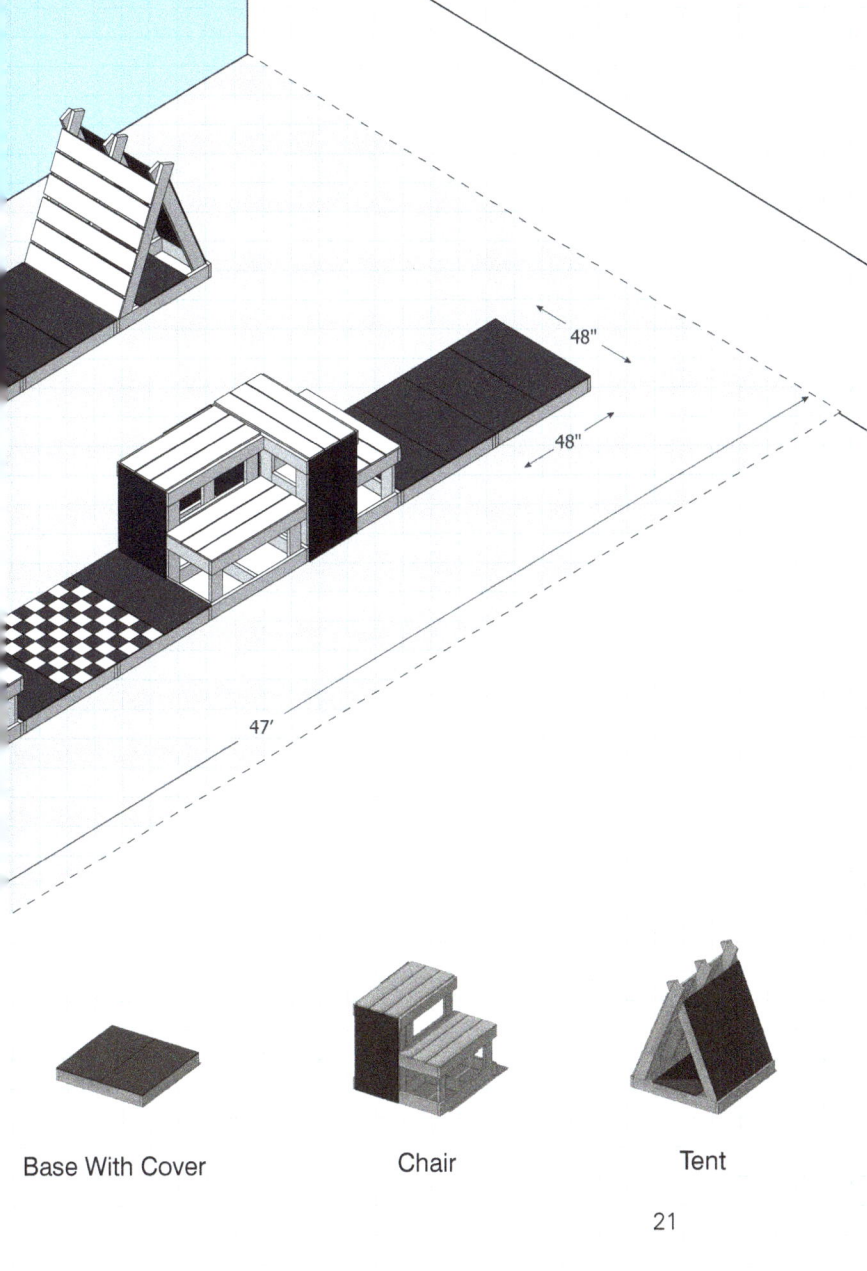

Base With Cover · Chair · Tent

PIECES

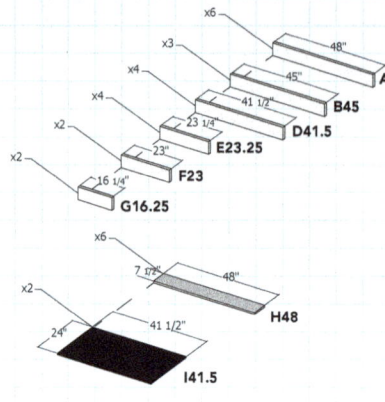

- A48 ×6 — 48"
- B45 ×3 — 45"
- D41.5 ×4 — 41 1/2"
- E23.25 ×4 — 23 1/4"
- F23 ×2 — 23"
- G16.25 ×2 — 16 1/4"
- H48 ×6 — 7 1/2" × 48"
- I41.5 ×2 — 24" × 41 1/2"

YOU WILL NEED

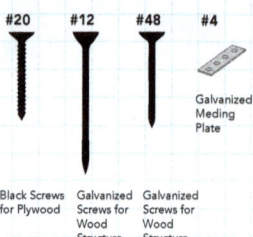

#20 Black Screws for Plywood
#12 Galvanized Screws for Wood Structure
#48 Galvanized Screws for Wood Structure [2" - 2 1/2"]
#4 Galvanized Mending Plate
#20 Galvanized Corner Brace

Pencil   Tape Measure
Paper Tape   Screwdriver

FRAME BASE

JOIN A48 + B45 AND THEN REPEAT.

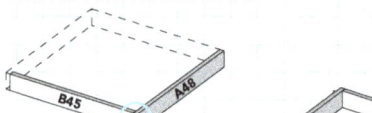
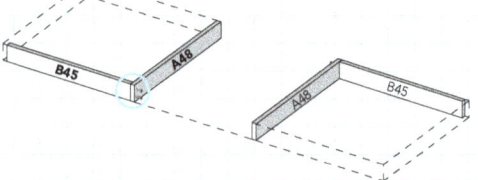

JOIN TWO "L" AS A SQUARE AND THEN ADD B45 IN THE MIDDLE.

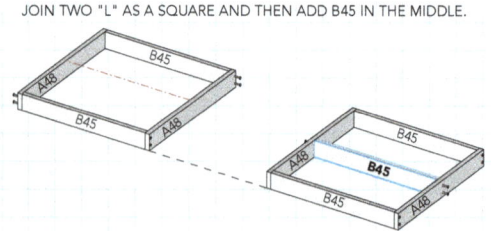

[DETAIL 01]

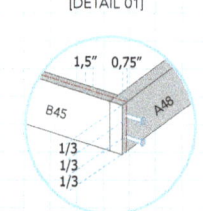

1,5" 0,75"
B45   A48
1/3
1/3
1/3

22

CHAIR

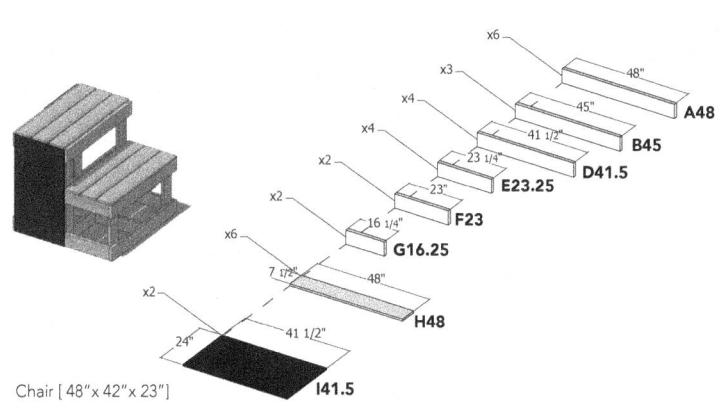

Chair [48"x 42"x 23"]

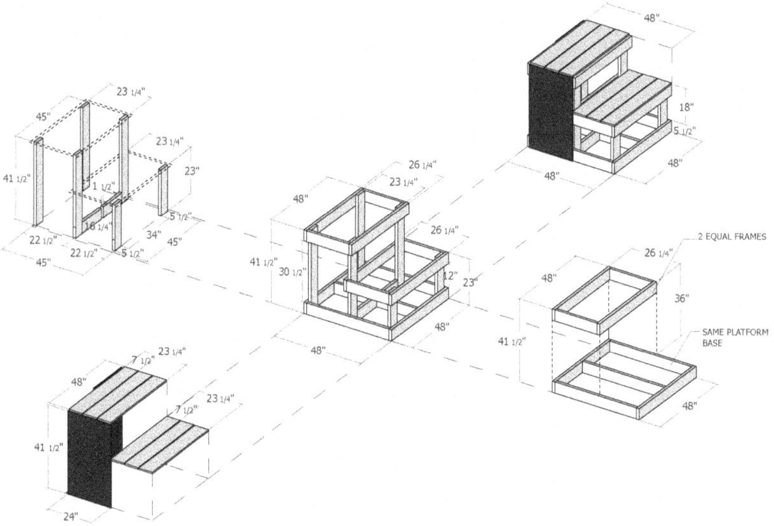

- A48 — x6 — 48"
- B45 — x3 — 45"
- D41.5 — x4 — 41 1/2"
- E23.25 — x4 — 23 1/4"
- F23 — x2 — 23"
- G16.25 — x2 — 16 1/4"
- H48 — x6 — 7 1/2" x 48"
- I41.5 — x2 — 24" x 41 1/2"

2 EQUAL FRAMES

SAME PLATFORM BASE

Community Building Workshop, October 2018

Chess For Kids, July 2019

Epilogue

Naomi Hersson-Ringskog, Newburgh resident and founder of the Dept of Small Interventions in conversation with **Kaja Kühl**, Hudson Valley Initiative

Naomi: What prompted you to do this project?

Kaja: In the summer of 2018, the Hudson Valley Initiative was asked by the City of Newburgh and Scenic Hudson to develop a "toolbox" or guide for improving city-owned vacant lots as part of a city-wide open space plan. When we discussed ideas for community engagement and how to involve residents in this process, our partners at the City felt that residents were tired of attending meetings and making plans without any visible signs of change. Instead, they suggested, we could choose one of five vacant sites to design and build a pop-up park as a pilot. Rather than verbal feedback at meetings, we could instead observe and ask, how the pilot would be used and accepted (or not) and develop the larger toolbox based on lessons learned. This was also a pilot for us in testing this method of working. As a community design initiative, we are used to a robust engagement process with a larg group of stakeholders. We did like the idea of thinking about engagement as "just being there," occupying the site, and asking people to help, but it was also new territory. No initial meetings, discussions, or consensus-building. No period of trust-building upfront. Of the five sites, we chose one at 191 South Street because we were interested in its potential to become a social space.

Naomi: Could you list the factors for selecting that site?

Kaja: The scale played a role and we were interested in collaborating with immediate neighbors such as the blacc vanilla coffee shop and the churches nearby. We always knew that not every site needs to be an active social space. Some could just be cleaned and nicer to look at without active use. But we thought that for a pilot, inviting active use and participation in creating the site would give us more insight in the community's appetite for this kind of open space.

Naomi: What were your general observations of the pilot?

Kaja: We certainly learned a lot that ultimately informed the content of the toolbox we developed for the city.[6] And most of it we would have not learned through more conventional community engagement. Going through the process of temporarily taking over government-owned land, even when the government recruited you to do so, can be a bit daunting, but also allowed us to experience first-hand what anyone who would want to replicate this project would have to do.

Naomi: What was the bureaucratic process for doing this on government -owned land?

Kaja: Newburgh City Planning and the City's Counsel had prepared a license agreement for us to sign that allowed us to use the land for one year. We had to present the idea and design at a City Council work session to receive approval for the project. There was a mix of concern and support among the City Council members. This happened during a time period when the Newburgh water crisis was very acute and several city officials had recently resigned.[7] So right when we needed guidance from the city, it was unclear who our point person was. The bigger hurdle turned out to be our own bureaucracy.

It took several weeks to find out who at Columbia University would have the authority to sign such an agreement.

Naomi: How did you come up with the design?

Kaja: While we always envisioned that some of the approximately 50 city-owned vacant lots could be passive "clean and green" sites, we wanted this pilot to be a social space. With the blacc vanilla coffee shop close by, we envisioned it as an outdoor overflow space and discussed the idea with blacc vanilla's owner. So we developed ideas for tables and seating. We also had initial conversations with the Newburgh Urban Farm and Food Initiative (NUFFI). But the site has no access to water and NUFFI didn't want to start another garden. Their goal is to empower others to start gardens. We knew we wouldn't be able to maintain a garden and had no committed partner to do so. The design we developed was a flexible system of open boxes, platforms and oversized seats, all based on the same dimensions. They could be combined in different arrangements and offer space for a picnic, a chessboard, some low-maintenance plants, a sandbox and space just to sit and enjoy the sun. Another criteria was a concern for vandalism and durability, also expressed by the City Council. As a result, we opted for heavy and inexpensive material. Unlike folding chairs and tables, these pieces couldn't be carried away easily. The plywood was painted in chalkboard paint that served as a playful opportunity to leave messages but also as water protection for the wood.

A third criteria was that it should be easy to build. We wanted to involve Newburgh residents in the construction process. Sofia Valdivieso, our designer, did a phenomenal job in drawing up instructions for how to put

the pieces together. Since almost everything was based on the same dimensions, we built the majority of it in one day together with volunteers.

That said, we had to improvise a bit. We didn't have enough material for some pieces and never completed the more detailed and aspirational aspects of the design. And this had repercussions. For instance, the original design called for a cover for the sandbox. This was never built because of budget and time constraints and as a result – as one could imagine– towards the later months of the summer, parents did not deem the sandbox a clean place to play.

Naomi: What can you share about the timeline of the project?

Kaja: Things always take longer than imagined. We started designing in June 2018. By the time we had approval from the City Council, had our insurance in place and a contractor who would help us build the park, it was September. Essentially we didn't get to fully complete and use the park until the following spring.

As a result, for the toolbox, we proposed a limited application window from January to April each year to ensure that projects can get off the ground and sites can be used during the summer months. It also helps the City to anticipate and plan for staff capacity during that time.

Naomi: Can you describe in more detail reactions to the space from the community?

Kaja: There are three interesting observations:

First, despite a sign that suggested that the park was open to the public, residents remained hesitant at first. "I don't want to trespass," one resident told us, unsure, whether he would be allowed to use the space. The sign was very stylish. Perhaps a simpler, but more obvious sign would have helped. But ultimately I think we learned that signage alone cannot replace the sense of belonging people feel for something they are a part of. Second, residents of surrounding blocks frequently sit together on the sidewalk in front of their houses to meet and chat. These informal meetings did not relocate to the pop-up park. We did observe that the park was used by different age groups throughout the summer, but it did not become a regular meeting spot or even the overflow area for blacc vanilla, as we had hoped.

And third, in a serendipitous way, which is the magic of community building, we met and encouraged the "Chess for Kids" program run by the Newburgh Armory Center to get involved in the project. They designed and painted an outdoor chessboard and chess figures for the space. The kids and their families would come regularly to the pop-up park on Sundays to play chess. This regular presence contributed positively to a sense of well-being and safety and to the maintenance of the park itself. We probably would have liked to see a few more regular users such as the chess kids.

Keep in mind though, as I mentioned earlier, not every space needs to become an active social space. Studies have shown that even just a simple clean up of a site can contribute positively to the well-being of residents. I also think there is a delicate balance to strike. A space that is "owned" and programmed by some can feel excluding to others. Do I feel welcome in a community garden, without the gardeners explicitly inviting me?

Lastly, I want to mention a very positive experience. While we worried about security and the potential for crime or vandalism, this turned out not to be the case. During the entire year, no complaints reached us or the city. Staff at blacc vanilla helped keep the site clean and a message suggesting the same on the park's sign encouraged users to contribute to the maintenance of the park. In a way this was very encouraging. People generally respected the work and care that went into creating the pop-up park.

Naomi: How is a project like this financed?

Kaja: The Hudson Valley Initiative donated time for design and project management. It's hard to put a price tag on this. Think of it as a big amount of volunteer labor, some of which would actually come much easier to a Newburgh resident with knowledge of place, people and the city's approval process, which was mostly new to us. Scenic Hudson donated $5,000 for material and construction of the pop-up park. This budget was definitely small for our local contractor and the design we envisioned. I do believe that you can have a similarly functioning space for less. You could just buy picnic tables and outdoor games and wouldn't have to involve a contractor for instance.

We used Columbia University's liability insurance for the duration of the project. This is another cost factor to keep in mind. The city will require anyone who signs a license agreement to take over a city-owned lot to provide insurance. For the toolbox, we asked a local insurance agent for a quote: approximately $1,000 per year.

Naomi: If you had to do it again, what would you do differently?

Kaja: First of all, be more realistic about timing and trust-building in the community. I would plan this as a long-term presence in the community, and not rush to get it built so quickly, but instead use earlier months for light programming and events on site . This would perhaps allow us to build stronger partnerships and be more transparent, especially with direct neighbors.

We hosted several meetings for discussion and feedback while the park was in place. With more patience, we could strive to slowly transition "ownership" to local partners, while maintaining the fiscal and legal responsibility for a little longer until there is enough capacity in the community for us to completely exit. That said, I hope Newburgh residents will make use of the toolbox and am excited about supporting them in transforming vacant lots into vibrant neighborhood spaces in the future.

References

1 Alan Mallach (2018): The Empty House Next Door: Understanding and Reducing Vacancy and Hypervacancy in the United States, Columbia University Press, New York

2 New York Land Bank Association (2019): Testimony For The Joint Legislative Hearing on Economic Development, NY State Senate, February 2019

3 Ignasi Sola-Moralez Rubio (1995): "Terrain Vague" in Anyplace, MIT Press, Cambridge MA

4 Downing Park, designed in 1889 was the last collaboration between Olmsted and Vaux, the designers responsible for New York City's Central Park among many other urban landscapes designed and built in the 19th century.

5 Branas CC, Kondo MC, Murphy SM, South EC, Polsky D, MacDonald JM (2016): "Urban blight remediation as a cost-beneficial solution to firearm violence" in American Journal of Public Health 106(10): 1-7,

6 The toolbox refers to "Lots of Ideas Newburgh - A Toolbox for Turning Vacant Lots into Vibrant Neighborhood Spaces", Hudson Valley Initiative, 2020.

7 Toxic chemicals known as PFAS (per and polyfluoroalkyl substances) were found to have contaminated Newburgh's primary reservoir, Lake Washington. Alternate sources of water have been provided to ensure tap water is running free of PFAS in the short term, but it is still unclear, how clean up and filtering of the reservoir water will ensure safe drinking water for the city.

Acknowledgment

The pilot was installed at 191 South Street in Newburgh, NY from October 2018 to October 2019 and was made possible through the generous support by Scenic Hudson.

Design Team:
Kaja Kühl
Sofia Valdivieso Fluxa
Whitney Bayer
Aura Maria Jamarillo

Thank you to:
Heather Blaikie, Ali Church, Melanie Collins,
AJ Dederick, Jackie Hesse (and the students at P-Tech),
Naomi Hersson-Ringskog, Amy Kacala, Jerrod Lang,
Matthew Tether (and the Newburgh Armory Chess Program)

Editor: Kaja Kühl

Photographs:
Kaja Kühl, Matthew Tether

© 2020 Hudson Valley Initiative, Columbia GSAPP

www.ingramcontent.com/pod-product-compliance
Lightning Source LLC
Chambersburg PA
CBHW050817090426
42736CB00022B/3487